FROM

CE

TO

E

FROM ACE TO ZE

An Hachette UK Company
www.hachette.co.uk

Summersdale Publishers Ltd
Part of Octopus Publishing Group Limited
Carmelite House
50 Victoria Embankment
LONDON
EC4Y 0DZ
UK

www.summersdale.com

Printed and bound in Malta

ISBN: 978-1-78685-284-7

Substantial discounts on bulk quantities of Summersdale books are available to corporations, professional associations and other organisations. For details contact general enquiries: telephone: +44 (0) 1243 771107 or email: enquiries@summersdale.com.

FROM ACE TO Z

THE LITTLE BOOK OF LGBT TERMS

HARRIET DYER

INTRODUCTION

Hello there. Welcome to this introduction to useful LGBTQ+ terminology. If you're an LGBTQ+ newbie, there can be a lot to get to grips with, especially as society still has a long way to go in representing everyone within it. Or perhaps you are involved in the community, but words and phrases gain subtleties as society develops and there may be a few areas of gender and sexuality you might want to know more about.

In this book I've tried to include the most up-to-date thinking on gender, sexuality and identity. If this book helps you understand a few new things, great! And if you read something that doesn't seem quite right to you, then please let me know at **auntie@summersdale.com**. Meanings develop all the time, so if I've got something wrong, I want to improve on it for next time.

Look, this isn't new stuff. Yes, the fact that so many people are discussing things like this openly is pretty new. But the identities aren't new. The feelings aren't new. The ways people want to identify and live and love aren't new. Make no mistake, people have been living and loving all sorts of ways since the beginning of people. We've just got a few more words to use now. And that's pretty cool.

LITTLE NOTE

LGBTQ+ has been used throughout. There are lots of great arguments in favour of using different variations of the acronym but for the purposes of ease and quick understanding, LGBTQ+ has been the acronym of choice in this introductory book.

SEX VS GENDER

At points you might feel like you need a dictionary just to read this dictionary! After all, although some phrases may be new to you, others will be words you learned at school but… not with the definitions you're familiar with? You might well be confused! Like I said in the introduction, this is all a learning process. To help you along the way, we're going to have a quick dive into one of the key questions you might have when reading this book: aren't sex and gender the same thing?! (Spoiler alert, no!) It's understandable how we may have developed this view. Sex is explored in dusty, easily forgotten biology classes, and we're never really taught much about gender at all. In casual conversation, sex and gender tend to be used interchangeably.

In fact, sex and gender do not have the same definition. Perhaps the easiest way to explain it is with this diagram:

 GENDER IDENTITY

 SEXUAL ORIENTATION

 PHYSICAL SEX

 GENDER EXPRESSION

Sex is a scientific term referring to your biology. Humans are generally catagorised into two sexes, **male** and **female** (for **intersex**, see P.66). Your sex is defined by sex characteristics, including genitals, sex organs, hormones and 'secondary' characteristics like height, weight and hair distribution. Although, to be honest, all that happens for those of us not born into a scientific study is that a medical professional will confirm your sex at birth by checking your genitals and then it's up to you to discover the rest as you get older. (For the full definition of sex, see P.104) Gender, on the other hand, is your *internal* experience of your identity. It's not what your body looks like or acts like, it's how you feel. Your **gender expression** (P.52) will reflect that. Society being as it is, there are informal checklists for this, too. For example, there are very few glamorous dresses in men's clothing departments. Throughout various cultures, some professions are thought to be 'masculine' and some to be 'feminine'. For an easy way to distinguish between the two, you could say that sex is the body and gender is the mind. Now, of course, it's possible to ask even more questions about sex and gender. There are entire academic careers built around exploring the definitions of sex and gender, in fact! For example, there are arguments that sex is also a social construct. If you're interested in learning more about this then it's definitely worthwhile reading up about it: see the back of this book for useful links, and a list of books that go into more detail than we have scope for in this dictionary! Because this book is trying to introduce as much as possible, it would be hard to delve deeper and still keep everything as accurate and clear as we'd like. Therefore, for the purposes of *From Ace to Ze*, we'll be keeping the definition of sex as a biological one.

ROMANCE VS SEXUALITY

Here's another distinction that's useful to have in mind when reading this book. Sex and romance aren't the same thing. I know, I know, this is the debate upon which a thousand groanworthy sitcoms and romcoms have hinged. But it simply isn't the same thing.

There are many people in the world who don't have to take into account the difference between romantic and sexual attraction. They experience romantic and sexual attraction at the same time, and often to one gender. For example, if someone were to identify themselves to you as heterosexual, they wouldn't usually go on to explain that they also felt *romantic* attraction towards people of a different sex. We'd take it for granted! And because there are so many people who experience romantic and sexual attraction as one, their voices tend to be the loudest. Because of this, we might assume that this is the case for everyone. But it's not!

For some of us, who we want to sleep with is different to who we want to be in a relationship with. For others, they don't want to sleep with anyone but they still want a sweetheart by their side. For yet others, a relationship isn't for them but they do enjoy an active sex life (or would like to). Because there are so many different ways a person can experience attraction, it's important to establish the distinctions from the start.

A quick guide is: sexual attraction is the desire to have sex or do sexy things with a person. Romantic attraction is an emotional attraction to another person, sometimes the desire to have a relationship with them. It's the hand-holding, date-going stuff.

As with the sex vs gender section, there are more subtleties and complexities than this book can hope to cover. If you think you want to learn more, please check the reading list and links at the back.

GENDER PRONOUNS

Sex, gender, love and romance; a few pages in and we've already tackled some of the biggest, bafflingest subjects out there. So instead of going bigger, let's go small. Let's look at some of the smallest, most frequently used words in the English language: pronouns.

Tiny but mighty, pronouns are some of the building blocks of language. They help us make clear who we're talking about; who said the thing, who did the thing, who is the thing. But the little habits and assumptions need to be challenged just as much as the big ideas.

The problem with our language is that many of its pronouns lock you into the gender **binary** (P.26). Him/Her doesn't adequately represent some people's gender expression. Even if someone does use the pronouns 'him' or 'her', if they're guessing their new acquaintance's gender they may guess wrong. It's a potential minefield, both for the person who doesn't wish to give offence and the person who is stuck having to correct an otherwise cool new friend in order to correct a misconception. But! There are ways around this!

One is using new gender-neutral pronouns, like **Ze** and **Zir** (P.122). Another is sticking to an old gender-neutral pronoun, *they*. (Grammar pedants won't like this but tough cookies because humans>grammar. Yes, I said it.) The third and best option is simply asking someone 'What are your pronouns?' when you meet them. Yes, it might feel awkward at first, but most new meetings *are* awkward. If you can survive the 'will we hug or handshake as hello' dilemma, you can survive using four words to make someone feel more comfortable.

If that still seems too fussy, why not take it back to good old-fashioned courtesy, where the first rule is kindness and treating others the way they wish to be treated?

A

ABROSEXUAL

Someone whose sexual orientation is not fixed, and changes often. It would not be accurate to say, for example, that an abrosexual person is gay one day and bisexual the next, as their sexual identity remains abrosexual. Instead, they would (for example) experience sexual attraction to people of the same gender as them one day and to people of other genders the next.

ACE

1. Short for **asexual** (P.23).

2. A person who identifies as asexual.

ACE SPECTRUM

The range of asexual identities. Because there isn't just one way to be asexual – to not feel and/or have never felt sexual attraction – it's useful to think of all sexuality as a ruler and asexuality as a set of points on that scale. For example, one person may rarely feel sexual attraction and only sometimes have sex, and identify as asexual. Another person may have never felt sexual attraction and identify as asexual. This may change over their lifetime, or remain the same. (See P.106 for **spectrum**.)

ACEFLUX/AROFLUX

A person who identifies on the ace spectrum. Their identity is fluid; their level of sexual attraction or urges is changeable.

AFFIRM

A positive confirmation that what has been said has been heard and believed. Affirmation is a word that has existing uses outside of the LGBTQ+ community but carries extra weight within the community. It not only signals hearing and understanding, but also that the words are welcome and accepted as truth. Many people within minority groups have experienced doubt and invalidation when sharing their stories. For example, 'love the sinner, hate the sin' or 'are you sure you can't just *not* be this way?' Half-acceptance like this hurts, so the act of affirmation is incredibly powerful.

AGENDER

Someone who does not identify as any particular gender; genderless.

ALLOROMANTIC

Someone who has the urge and/or inclination to have romantic relationships with other people.

ALLOSEXUAL

Someone who has sexual urges and feels sexual attraction towards other people. This can be a useful term that identifies the other end of the spectrum to **asexuality** (P.23). Identifying and naming opposite sexuality helps to move thinking from 'normal libido vs asexual libido', which implies the asexual drive is abnormal or **other** (P.86), to 'we are all related on the sexual spectrum'.

ALLY

A person who supports a group without being part of that group themselves.

ANDROGYNE

1. A person who is ambiguously gendered. This is actually the older form of the word androgynous (opposite). As with all identities, androgynes operate on a spectrum. All experience a mix of genders, some who identify as more man than woman, others more woman than man and yet others who may identify as entirely neutral.

2. Someone who presents as ambiguously gendered. This is their **gender expression** (see P.52) and may not reflect their gender identity. For example, someone may identify as a woman and choose to style themselves ambiguously with clothes, hair, make-up, etc.

ANDROGYNEROMANTIC

Romantic attraction to people who are androgynous.

ANDROGYNESEXUAL

Sexual attraction to people who are androgynous.

ANDROGYNOUS

Ambiguously gendered in appearance. This can refer to physical characteristics such as hair or build and also gender expression, such as clothes or make-up.

APORAGENDER

Apora is from the Greek *apor*, meaning separate, so can be translated as 'separate gender'. Aporagender people have a strong feeling that they are gendered, while not identifying as male, female or any gender between those two on the gender spectrum.

APPROPRIATION

Taking something from a culture from which one did not originate and using it without proper thought, credit or permission. A common example of this is when a white person wears a Native American headdress to a festival; although it's intended as fun dress up, Native American headdresses have religious or spiritual meanings and are intended to be worn by specific tribes, in specific circumstances and/or by specific people.

ARO

1. Short for aromantic.

2. Someone who identifies on the aromantic spectrum.

AROMANTIC

Someone who does not feel the urge or inclination to be in a romantic relationship with other people. An aromantic person may identify as sexual and enjoy sexual relationships.

ASEXUAL

Someone who does not usually feel sexual attraction or a sexual urge towards other people.

Asexuality works on a spectrum, like sexuality; some people who consider themselves to be asexual never feel sexual attraction or urges; others do on occasion. Some are averse to any sexual touch or interaction, others engage in it on occasion to please their partners or themselves. An asexual identity doesn't have to stem from a revulsion against sex; some asexual identities simply don't find sex interesting, fulfilling or important.

BI-ERASURE

The act of belittling, demeaning or obscuring the existence of bisexual people.

Common biphobic assumptions include that if a man comes out as bisexual it is a stepping stone to 'admitting' he is gay, and that if a woman comes out as bisexual she is straight and 'experimenting' for (usually male) attention. Bi-erasure can also take place in academic debate, such as when discussing a famous or historical figure and debating their sexuality; if the debate centres around the figure being straight or gay without considering bisexuality, that is bi-erasure.

BIGENDER

Someone who identifies as two genders. This could be as both male and female, or two genders across the gender spectrum. These identities can be distinct, so the person only experiences one gender at a time, but two genders in total. Or the person could identify as two genders at once.

BINARY

A system of identification involving only two things. One example is the gender binary; male/man **or** female/woman.

BIPHOBIA

A prejudice against bisexual people.

BIROMANTIC

Romantic feelings and the desire to be in a relationship with either male or female people.

BISEXUAL

Sexual attraction towards people of the same gender as well as people of other genders. Often used as an umbrella term to include biromanticism, although some bisexual people have sexual urges towards both male or female people but prefer to only be in romantic relationships with either male or female people.

CAFAB

Initialism; coercively assigned female at birth. A lot of terminology is about challenging our assumptions. CAFAB and **CAMAB** (below) acknowledge that the person isn't able to communicate their gender at birth, and that the choice was made for them without their consent, in this case incorrectly. This is helpful in shifting the **trans** (P.109) narrative from the incorrect 'changing from one gender to another' to 'expressing your true gender'.

CAMAB

Initialism; coercively assigned male at birth. (See above.)

CISGENDER

A cisgender person is one whose assigned-at-birth gender matches their gender identity.

Using this term avoids establishing a default or 'normal' and acknowledges that everyone has a relationship between their birth gender and gender identification.

CLOSETED (IN THE CLOSET)

A slang term for when a person identifies as LGBTQ+ but has not shared this aspect of their identity with friends, family or their wider community. This is sometimes used derogatorily, but there can be many reasons a person chooses to not reveal part of their identity, the key reason being safety.

COMING OUT

When a person shares their LGBTQ+ identity with friends, family or their wider community.

The phrase is thought to have originated in the early twentieth century in America. Young upper-class women would be formally presented in society to indicate their families now viewed them as adults. This was referred to as 'coming out'. Originally the phrase was used by LGBTQ+ people to indicate that they were coming out into gay society or identity.

Now 'coming out' more commonly refers to coming out of the **closet** (P.31).

COMMUNITY

A group who have something in common. Community is an umbrella term for LGBTQ+ people, activists, organisations and their supporters. Although not all LGBTQ+ people consider themselves as part of the community, generally the community is seen as a supportive environment, encouraging diversity, individuality, identity and sexuality.

CONFLATE

The combination of two ideas or concepts into one. For example, 'Sexuality and gender are often conflated, although they are separate issues.'

D

DEADNAMING

The use of a transgender or **genderqueer** (P.57) person's birth name, if they have not kept that name on transitioning. Using the 'dead' name can be hurtful, as it ignores the person's chosen name and often misgenders them.

DEMIGENDER

An umbrella term for gender identities where someone feels only a partial connection to a gender identity or even gender itself. A person who identifies as demigender may identify with one or more genders.

DEMIMAN

A person whose gender identity is mainly, but not completely, male. Some feel that their identity is also in part another gender, others identify only with a male gender identity.

DEMIROMANTIC

Someone who only feels romantic attraction to people with whom they have formed a strong emotional connection. The 'demi' of demiromantic and **demisexual** (opposite) indicates that the attraction or sexuality is halfway between **aromantic/asexual** (PP.22-23) and **alloromantic/allosexual** (P.18).

DEMISEXUAL

Someone who only feels sexual attraction to people with whom they have formed a strong emotional connection.

Here it seems important to clarify a few things. Many of us live in a society that has a lot of messy assumptions about sex (and particularly in regards to gender) and one of those assumptions might be that it is somehow 'better' to not have sex until you know someone well, regardless of your preference. Of course, it is in fact always 'better' to have sex at the point that you wish to have it, with the person you wish to have it with and who wishes to have it with you. However, it isn't that demisexuals are choosing to not have sex until they know someone well; they in fact do not experience sexual attraction until they have formed an emotional bond with someone.

DEMIWOMAN

A person whose gender identity is mainly, but not, completely female. Some feel that their identity is also in part another gender, others identify only with a female gender identity.

DFAB

Initialism meaning 'designated female at birth'. Similar terms include AFAB (assigned female at birth) and FAAB (female assigned at birth). (See P.29 for **coercively assigned X at birth**.)

DIOMORIC

1. A person whose gender identity is non-binary and who's attracted to relationships with other non-binary people.

2. A relationship or attraction in which one or more of the participants are non-binary.

DMAB

Initialism meaning 'designated male at birth'. Similar terms include AMAB (assigned male at birth) and MAAB (male assigned at birth). (See P.29 for **coercively assigned X at birth**.)

DYSPHORIA

The feeling of discomfort or unease. Gender dysphoria is the feeling that your body's gender doesn't match your true gender. People with gender dysphoria often feel trapped inside a body that isn't 'theirs'.

ENBIAN

1. A person whose gender identity is **non-binary** (P.81) and who's attracted to relationships with other non-binary people.

2. A relationship or attraction in which all participants are non-binary.

ENBY

Slang, a non-binary person (from the initials, N.B.).

ERASURE

The total removal of something.

The act of ignoring an individual or group's existence or right to exist, or insufficiently representing them or taking them into account. Usually as a result of prejudice, whether conscious or unconscious. For example, if you claimed your portrayal of the Stonewall riots was based in reality but didn't include the transwomen and LGBTQ+ people of colour who were historically recorded as involved, you would be perpetrating an act of erasure against them. Erasure is especially damaging as it often takes place in media portrayals of society which people often take to be truthful, leading people to believe that minority people really weren't present in these situations, and indeed that certain minorities are barely present in society.

FEMALE TO FEMALE

An identifier, indicating that a person has transitioned from their assigned birth sex of male to their true gender of female. By using 'female to female' instead of 'male to female' the person rejects that their gender was ever male. As with abbreviations such as **CAMAB** (P.29), these terminology readjustments help change the trans narrative to something that affirms their identity.

FEMALE TO MALE

An identifier, indicating that a person has transitioned/is transitioning from their assigned birth sex of female to their true gender of male.

-FLEXIBLE

A suffix usually attached to a gender or sexual identity term, indicating that someone's identity is not fixed or moves within the spectrum. For example, one of the most common uses is heteroflexible, where a person identifies as mostly heterosexual but also experiences urges or takes part in sexy acts with other genders (usually not very often). Heteroflexible identities move on the heterosexual spectrum.

-FLUID

Not fixed, able or likely to change.

When this suffix is attached to a gender or identity term, it indicates that the identity is not fixed and moves within the spectrum it exists on. The fluidity of an identity can be felt at random or in response to certain circumstances. It can also be weighted more to one area of the spectrum or can fluctuate evenly between different identities. E.g. most commonly used with gender as 'genderfluid'.

-FLUX

A suffix usually attached to a gender or sexual identity term, indicating that someone's identity is not fixed or moves within the spectrum. See **aroflux** (P.16).

FTF

Initialism; **female to female**. (P.44)

FTM

Initialism; **female to male**. (P.44)

GAY

Homosexual. Can refer to people of any gender identity but is most commonly used to refer to homosexual men.

GENDER

A social system of classification.

Gender can be defined by several factors: biological sex, social structures (such as **gender roles**, see P.56) and gender identity (see **sex vs gender,** P.6). A person might choose to use one, several or all of these factors to define their gender. Gender classification is rooted in societal ideas about masculinity and femininity, and most gender identities are based on those two points, but there are gender identities that reject masculinity and femininity and stand outside of those.

GENDER CONFUSION/ GENDER FUCK

A way of presenting yourself that deliberately plays with gender.

GENDER DYSPHORIA

A feeling of discomfort, that your assigned gender doesn't match your true gender. See P.39 for more in-depth discussion.

GENDER EUPHORIA

A feeling of ecstatic happiness and peace with your gender identity and expression.

GENDER EXPRESSION

How an individual chooses to display or show their gender. This could be through appearance, actions, how they speak or various other factors.

Society is a funny thing. When you think about it, it seems strange to realise that almost everything you do, appearance-wise, is a form of gender expression. Changing anything about yourself to be outside of the gender norm can invite **policing** (P.92) from friends and strangers alike. Haircuts, make-up or no make-up, clothes and shoes are all unofficially categorised as masculine or feminine*. Ways of walking, tones or voice inflections and physical gestures all have gendered implications; even some professions are thought to be more suited to one gender than another. Almost every element of your life is gender expression.

*I'm using the gender binary here as that's the structure most societies have built their gender norms around.

GENDER IDENTITY

The internal sense of a person's gender. Put simply, how you feel in regards to your gender.

Gender identity is different to your sex, which is based on biology. So a transman's gender identity is male, but he was assigned female at birth. Separating gender and sex lets us paint a more accurate picture of the trans experience; a person doesn't change gender, as they were that gender since birth; however, they may choose to medically alter their sex to bring it in line with their gender identity.

GENDER INDIFFERENT

An identification where the person is uninterested in their gender identity.

GENDER-NEUTRAL

1. An identification where a person does not identify as one gender more than any other gender.

2. Something which is not about or intended for one gender over another. Gender neutrality can be useful in all sorts of ways. One example is its increasing usage in job titles – for example, fire officer instead of firewoman or fireman (it's unlikely the gender of the person putting out your fire will matter in the heat of the moment). Another is toys for children; campaigners have argued against the segregation of toys by gender, saying that it's up to the child to decide and that some children might get gender policed just because they don't play with the 'right' toy.

GENDER NONCONFORMING

An umbrella term for any gender identities that do not match society's gender norms, i.e. male or female. Other terms for this include gender diverse, gender variant and gender-expansive.

GENDER ROLES

Societal expectations about how different genders, usually male and female, should act.

These expectations can include jobs, hobbies, personality and physical attributes. For example, you may be able to sort the following list into 'masculine' or 'feminine' attributes*: long hair, doctor, knitting fanatic, leader. Academics within social sciences are studying gender roles to see if people are naturally inclined to them or if society has conditioned them to behave or look a certain way.

*We are using the most common gender identities here as most people will have been socialised to think of gender roles in the context of the gender binary.

GENDERFLUID

Someone who has no fixed identity within the gender spectrum. They may identify as a different gender from one day to the next. Your gender identity would not have to change on a daily basis to identify as genderfluid; you may feel different from week to week or month to month, etc.

GENDERFLUX

Someone who has no fixed identity within the gender spectrum. They may identify as a different gender from one day to the next.

GENDERQUEER

An umbrella term for a person whose gender identity is not binary.

GREYROMANTIC

Someone who sometimes feels inclined towards romantic relationships and sometimes does not.

GREYSEXUAL

Someone who sometimes feels sexual attraction and urges and sometimes does not.

GSRM

An initialism standing for 'gender, sexual and romantic minorities'.

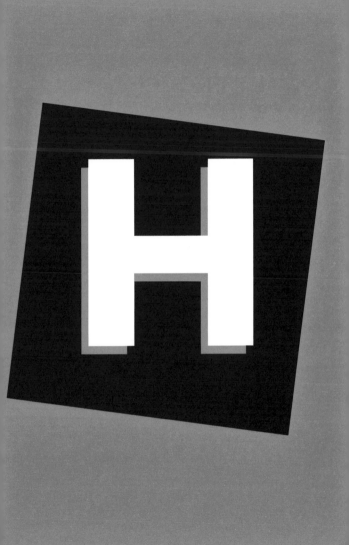

HETEROCENTRISM

The assumption that all people are heterosexual.

We see heterocentrism within society in all sorts of ways. Working on an assumption that everyone is straight means that LGBTQ+ people are often forced into a situation where they have to either explain their identity or not share important parts of their life. For example, it's heterocentric to ask a new male friend whether he has a girlfriend or for a doctor to assume that because a woman is sexually active she could get pregnant. Being socially aware doesn't mean you can't have a good gossip with your buds or a doctor can't give out medical advice but a little mental realignment is helpful to ensure these conversations are as inclusive as possible!

HETEROROMANTIC

A preference for romantic relationships with people of a different gender. A person may experience sexual desire for and engage in sexual acts with people of the same gender, but still prefer to engage in romantic relationships solely with a person of a different gender.

HETEROSEXUAL

A sexual preference for people of a different gender. Commonly used as an umbrella term for a preference for romantic as well as sexual relationships with people of a different gender.

HOMOPHOBIA

A prejudice against or dislike of homosexual people.

HOMOROMANTIC

A preference for romantic relationships with people of the same gender. A person may experience sexual desire for and engage in sexual acts with people of other genders, but still prefer to engage in romantic relationships solely with a person of the same gender.

HOMOSEXUAL

A sexual preference for people of the same gender. Like **heterosexual** (P.61), this is one that has come to mean an all-round preference for people of the same gender, rather than just sexy feelings. As with some other words in this book, like **allosexual** (P.18), this one is a bit clinical for everyday use. When you use it in reference to people it can sound like you're categorising them. It's often better to use 'gay' or 'lesbian' where those words apply. Of course, as with all terms in this book, personal preference rules all! If a person you're talking to prefers 'homosexual' to any other term, then use that one!

IAFAB

Initialism, standing for 'intersex assigned female at birth'.

IAMAB

Initialism, standing for 'intersex assigned male at birth'.

ID

Slang, short for identify. For example, 'I ID as demisexual.'

INTERGENDER

A gender identity where a person identifies as a mix of the binary genders.

INTERNALISATION

The learning of attitudes or behaviours until those attitudes or behaviours become part of one's nature. Learning can be conscious or unconscious. For example, some social scientists believe that gender roles are internalised as you grow up.

INTERSECTIONALITY

The connection between social categories such as sexuality, gender, race and socio-economic status. When these categories overlap they create a new category that might change a person's experience of the world. So, just as someone who is wealthy might have a different life experience to someone who is poor, someone who is wealthy and straight might have a different experience to someone who is wealthy and LGBTQ+.

INTERSEX

A person who is born with sex characteristics that do not wholly belong in either category of male or female.

Sex characteristics can include genitals, hormones, chromosomes or gonads (slang for testicles but this is the biological term for ovaries too). Some intersex babies and children are surgically or hormonally altered so they have 'socially acceptable' sex characteristics. However, this is increasingly being seen as a human rights violation. Some intersex babies are assigned a gender at birth and raised as that gender; some later assign their own gender and others continue to identify as that gender.

LESBIAN

A woman who is sexually and romantically attracted to other women.

LGBTQIA+

An umbrella initialism that groups together the members of the queer community.

The 'true' definition of the initialism, and which letters should be included, is highly debated. One common definition is:

L – Lesbian
G – Gay
B – Bisexual
T – Transgender
Q – Queer
I – Intersex
A – Asexual
+ – a shorthand way to round up other queer identities to be included, such as pansexual or polyamorous.

For example, some trans activists question whether 'transgender' has a place within the initialism, as it is a gender identity rather than a sexual identity. Some people argue that being grouped with sexual identities contributes to misconceptions about trans identities, chiefly that being transgender is related to your sexuality. There are arguments in favour of transgender staying as the 'T' in 'LGBTQ+' too; for many the experience of exploring their gender identity and their sexual identity share many similarities, such as coming out or experiencing pressure to conform to societal norms. The identities contained in the +, such as pansexual, are a varied mix, relating to both gender and sexual identity.

LIBIDO

The drive or urge to have sex, whether alone or partnered.

LIBIDOIST

A person who has a sex drive, but does not experience sexual attraction or urges towards other people. Sometimes referred to as libidoist asexual or under the umbrella term of asexual.

LITHROMANTIC

A romantic identity where a person can feel romantic attraction, but does not seek reciprocation or a romantic relationship. Some lithromantics enjoy a theoretical or fantasy romantic relationship.

MALE TO FEMALE

An identifier, indicating that a person has transitioned/is transitioning from their assigned sex of male to their true gender of female.

MALE TO MALE

An identifier, indicating that a person has transitioned from their assigned sex of female to their true gender of male.

By using 'male to male' instead of 'female to male' the person rejects that their gender was ever female. This terminology allows a subtle but important shift in thinking, from the idea that a person changes from one gender to another to the idea that a person is always the gender they identify as, but may choose to alter their sex characteristics to more accurately represent that gender.

MONOROMANTICISM

Romantic attraction to and the urge to have romantic relationships with only one gender. A person who is monoromantic may be sexually attracted to more than one gender but only romantically attracted to one.

MONOSEXUALITY

Sexual attraction to one gender.

MTF

An initialism, standing for '**male to female**' (P.73).

MTM

An initialism, standing for '**male to male**' (P.74).

MULTIGENDER

A gender identity where a person identifies as more than one gender.

MULTISEXUALITY

Sexual attraction to more than one gender.

NEUTROIS

A person whose gender identity is neutral. They identify as neither male nor female, a mix of the two or a different gender that is neither male nor female. Other terms similar to neutrois are **agender** (P.17) and genderless.

NOMAROMANTIC

A person who is romantically attracted to and/or wishes to be in a romantic relationship with anyone who isn't a man. The term is derived from the words 'no man romantic'.

NOMASEXUAL

Sexual urges and attraction towards anyone who isn't a man. A person who identifies as nomasexual might feel sexual attraction to women and also non-binary people.

NON-BINARY

Someone who is not defined by a system of identification involving only two things.

Of the gender and sexual identities included in this book, the ones that are probably the most well-known are those that involve the binary: male, female, gay and straight. Non-binary identities are any that exist outside of male **or** female, gay **or** straight and instead include identities that are neither, partially or a combination of these things. For example, **genderfluid** (see P.57) is a non-binary identity.

NORMALISE

When something becomes an accepted part of society. There are many ways in which you can measure whether something is an accepted part of society. One of the big ones that we keep mentioning here is media representation: is there a good mix of morally good and bad LGBTQ+ characters on TV?; does a photo-heavy article exploring family show pictures of LGBTQ+ families?; does a newspaper treat the subject of a celebrity's same sex partner in the same way it does other partners? We can look at other factors too, such as whether it's safe for everybody to express their identity in public.

NORMS

Societal customs and expectations. These are often unwritten rules of behaviour that indicate what is acceptable and what isn't. Unfortunately, these can be used to **police** (P.92) those who don't conform. For example, a (mostly) pleasant norm is to form a queue when more than a few people are waiting for something. A brisk tut if someone jumps the queue helps to enforce the norm. However, a gender norm is that boys don't play with doll babies. Sometimes this may be enforced by an adult ridiculing the child or taking the toy away, which, even done with kindness or ignorance, might be upsetting.

NOVOROMANTIC

A person whose romantic attractions are different depending on the gender they identify as at the time.

NOVOSEXUAL

A person whose sexual identity is different depending on the gender they identify as at the time. Novosexuals' gender and sexual identity are both fluid.

NOWOMAROMANTIC

A person who is romantically attracted to and/ or wishes to be in a romantic relationship with anyone who isn't a woman. The term is derived from the words 'no woman romantic'.

NOWOMASEXUAL

Sexual urges and attraction towards anyone who isn't a woman. A person who identifies as nowomasexual might feel sexual attraction to men and also non-binary people.

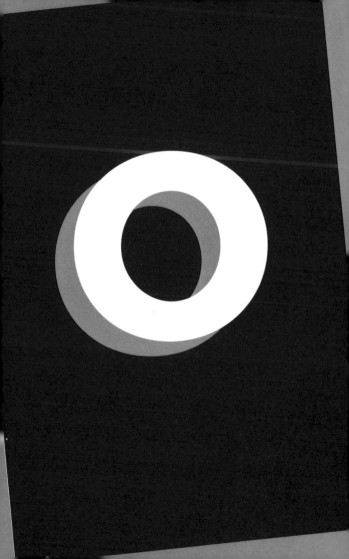

OMNIGENDER

A person whose gender identity consists of many or all genders.

OTHERING

Treating a person or behaviour that is different to your own as a person or behaviour that is abnormal.

OUT

When a person has disclosed their sexual or gender identity to friends/family/colleagues, etc.

For the origins of this phrase see P.32. Some people might choose to be selectively out, open with their gender or sexual identity to people they're close to and closeted to people they are not. For example, a person may decide not to be out at work because they don't wish to share their personal life with colleagues. Another person may choose to not be out at home as they are still a child and would be in a vulnerable position should their family know and disagree with their sexual or gender identity.

OUTING

The non-consensual reveal of a person's gender or sexual identity by someone other than themselves.

PANGENDER

A person whose gender identity consists of many or all genders.

PANROMANTIC

A person who is romantically attracted to and wishes to have relationships with people of any gender.

PANSEXUAL

A person who has sexual urges towards and is sexually attracted to people of any gender.

At first glance the definition of pansexual is the same as that of bisexual. However, the use of the word 'pan' is intended to open up the definition past the binary 'attracted to men and women' of bisexual and include attraction to people who appear anywhere on the gender spectrum. Not everyone agrees that the bisexual identity has those limitations on gender identity: ultimately personal choice is the decision-maker when it comes to the language you choose to identify yourself.

POLICING

When someone imposes limits on another person, usually in relation to gender or sexuality. The limits are usually based on societal norms, for example telling a father he can't be a stay-at-home-parent because he's a man.

POLYAMORY

A relationship consisting of more than two participants or the lifestyle in which someone could have multiple partners at the same time.

A polyamorous relationship can take many forms, depending on the desires of the participants. However, a polyamorous relationship is only such if all parties involved have all the information they wish to and have consented. Some polyamorous relationship structures include:

All parties are equally involved with each other: Persons A, B and C are in a throuple.

One participant is monogamous and the other has more than one relationship: Person A is in a relationship with B, B is in a relationship with A and C.

There are two 'primary' partners who have short-term or less prioritised relationships with other people: Person A is living with Person B; A sees C once a week and B spends two nights a week with D.

There are two participants who are primarily committed to each other but sleep with other people and either share or do not share details with each other.

There are of course many more ways to be polyamorous – it depends on what suits you and your partners.

POLYROMANTIC

Romantic attraction to or the desire to be in a relationship with more than one gender. More commonly referred to under the term **polyamory** (P.92).

POLYSEXUAL

Sexual urges towards and attraction to more than one gender.

PRIVILEGE

When rights, priorities or special attention is given to one person or group and not others. A person who experiences privilege may not be aware of it or may be disadvantaged in other ways, but despite this they are still privileged. For example, foundation for white skin tones is readily available in a range of shades and prices in most cosmetic shops, but foundation for other ethnicities is not. The ease of access in terms of both availability and affordability is a white privilege.

PRONOUN

A word used to refer to a person or object when their name is not used. Pronouns for humans are usually gendered, although there are some genderless pronouns in existence (P.122).

QUEER

An umbrella term for sexual and gender identities that are not heterosexual or cisgender (P.30).

The word queer has a long and storied use with regards to sexual and gender minorities. For a long time it was used as an insult for non-heterosexual people, but around the 1980s academics and people in the LGBTQ+ community started to reclaim it. It's now considered a useful umbrella term that handily encompasses many non-conforming genders and sexualities. Some prefer it to LGBTQ+ because unlike the initialism, it doesn't name identities, which is seen by some as a way to prioritise some identities over others, or to unnecessarily acknowledge the gender/sexuality binary.

QUEER STUDIES

Studies centring on the LGBTQ+ experience. Queer studies can involve many fields, including but not limited to literary theory, biology, psychology and history.

QUEERPLATONIC

A close but non-sexual, non-romantic relationship that is beyond what most would consider to be friendship. It consists of emotional commitment and prioritisation that may usually be seen in a romantic relationship. People in queerplatonic relationships may be of any gender or sexual identity.

QUESTIONING

When a person is unsure of their sexual or gender identity.

QUOIROMANTIC

When a person is unsure if they experience romantic attraction and the urge to be in a romantic relationship, or not.

QUOISEXUAL

When a person is unsure if they experience sexual attraction or the urge for sexual activity, or not.

R

RECIPROMANTICISM

When a person only experiences romantic attraction or wishes to be in a romantic relationship once they learn the person is interested in them.

RECIPSEXUALITY/ RECIPROSEXUALITY

When a person only experiences sexual attraction or sexual urges once they learn the person is interested in them.

SAME-GENDER LOVING

Sexual attraction to and the urge to have romantic relationships with people of the same gender.

This is an Afrocentric alternative to the words 'gay' and 'lesbian', coined by African–American activist Cleo Manago, and is gaining in popularity. Using different terminology highlights that the experience within the community can vary depending on your skin colour. The words 'gay' and 'lesbian' also grew out of white western history and, for some people of colour, the words don't engage with their experience.

SELF-IDENTIFICATION

The act of knowing or experiencing your gender and sexual identity.

SEX

1. A classification system using biological requirements, including sex chromosomes, gonads, internal genitalia, external genitalia and secondary sex characteristics such as height or hair distribution. See the introduction for more details, (P.6).

2. Intercourse! Sexy fun times. Doing the do, making love. Getting it on, having it off, going down. You get the idea!

SEX/GENDER ASSIGNMENT

The labelling of a human infant as male or female at birth based on their genitals. Trans and gender activists argue that this does not take into account gender identity. This means the label is non-consensual and can be wrongly assigned.

SGL

Initialism for **same-gender loving** (P.103).

SKOLIOROMANTIC

A sexual identity where a person is romantically attracted to people of non-binary or trans genders.

SKOLIOSEXUAL

A sexual identity where a person is sexually attracted to people of non-binary or trans genders.

SPECTRUM

A range.

Pioneering sexologist (yes, that's a job) Alfred Kinsey popularised the concept of using a spectrum to help people define sexuality with his Kinsey Scale in 1943, which measured hetero- and homosexual identities on a scale from 0–10. The Klein Sexual Orientation Grid built on this idea by introducing an XY axis that took into account asexuality and Storms' model developed a few years later with a grid that took into account how sexuality may change over time. There are currently over 200 scales measuring sexual orientation.

STIGMA

Societal prejudice and distaste towards a person, group, identity, act or behaviour.

TRANSFEMININE

Transgender people who were assigned male at birth, but identify on the gender spectrum as feminine. An umbrella term that refers to transwomen but also includes genderfluid people who identify as a woman most often, multigender people who identify as a woman most strongly, a demiwoman or any other primarily feminine non-binary gender identity.

TRANSGENDER

Someone whose true gender is different to the gender they were assigned at birth based on their sex.

This can mean they are gender binary; they were assigned male/female at birth and identify as female/male. Or they might identify as genderfluid and their body does not fully represent their gender identity. As gender is an internal experience and not a person's sex characteristics, someone might identify as transgender and have only partial or no surgery to alter their sex characteristics.

A commonly used abbreviation for transgender is 'trans'.

TRANSITION

The process of affirming a person's true gender, sometimes altering appearance, medically or surgically changing their body, changing their name or any other action they take to alleviate **dysphoria** (P.39).

TRANSMAN

A person who was assigned female at birth, but whose true gender is male.

TRANSMASCULINE

Transgender people who were assigned female at birth, but identify on the gender spectrum as masculine. An umbrella term that refers to transmen but also includes genderfluid people who identify as a man most often, multigender people who identify as a man most strongly, a demiman or any other primarily masculine non-binary gender identity.

TRANSSEXUAL

Transgender. Although the word is considered old fashioned and for many, offensive, some people identify with it by personal choice. By using the word 'sexual' it technically specifically refers to those who medically change their sex characteristics, even though it's mostly used as an umbrella term for people who identify as transgender. As gender identity is different to sex identity (see **gender identity** on P.53), this has led to its relative disuse in the transgender community.

TRANSWOMAN

A person who was assigned male at birth, but whose true gender is female.

TRIGENDER

A genderfluid identity that goes beyond binary gender identity (varying between male or female), literally 'three genders'.

TRIROMANTIC

Romantic attraction to three genders.

TRISEXUAL

Sexual attraction to three genders.

TRYROMANTIC

Having no or few initial romantic limits; very open to experimenting. This can refer to anything that usually informs romantic interest, from gender to number of partners, e.g. monogamy, **polyamory** (P.92), etc. Usually used as a 'joke' when expressing romantic or sexual identity.

TRYSEXUAL

Having no or few initial sexual limits; only deciding what you do not enjoy sexually after having experienced it. This can refer to anything that usually informs sexual interest, from gender to individual sex acts. Often used humorously, but is also a sexual identity.

UMBRELLA TERM

A word or phrase that gathers related terms into one group.

LGBTQ+ and its associated initialism is a famous umbrella term; it's a way to denote a community with many things in common. However, umbrella terms don't always work best for everyone; you can, for example, sometimes accidentally include someone who doesn't consider themself to be a part of that group. As with all the terminology in this book, someone's self-defined identity trumps your assessment of them. These things considered, umbrella terms are a handy shortcut when discussing things as complex and varied as gender or sexuality.

VALIDATE

To support the accuracy and truth of something.

One of the dictionary definitions of 'validate' is to verify or check the story. When it comes to validation in the LGBTQ+ community, validate has a slightly different meaning. The idea is to respect a person's story, accept that what they are saying is true and that their feelings on the matter they are discussing are genuine. It might seem a bit like basic advice to say 'assume that people aren't liars', but people in the LGBTQ+ community face a lot of questions and doubt about their self-reported experiences and it's useful to counter that where possible.

W

WLW

Short for 'women loving women'.
   Women who are sexually and romantically attracted to women.

WOMAN

Someone who identifies as female.

WOMAROMANTICISM

Romantic attraction to someone who is female.

WOMASEXUALITY

Sexual attraction to someone who is female.

WOMEN LOVING WOMEN

Women who are sexually and romantically attracted to women. Originated in the USA by women of colour who would prefer not to use the term 'lesbian'. Can also be used as a blanket term for women who identify as lesbian, bisexual and pansexual.

Z

ZE/ZIR

Gender-neutral pronouns.

Ze is the subjective case e.g, 'Ze ran all the way to the bus.' Zir is the possessive case: 'Zir eyes were brown' and the objective case: 'I accidentally butt-dialled Zir.' These might be used when referring to genderqueer people who prefer to not use gendered pronouns or when you're unsure of someone's pronouns. One option is to use a pronoun that's already in common usage, 'they'. There are other forms of gender-neutral pronouns: ne/nem/nirs, ve/ver/vis, ey/em/eir or xe/xem/xir. There is no definitive guideline yet on which would be the best to use; if deciding on what's best for yourself you could simply choose your favourite, and if deciding on what to use for other people it's generally best to ask 'what are your pronouns?' and use their preference.

ZEDROMANTIC

Someone who has the urge and inclination to have romantic relationships with other people.

ZEDSEXUAL

Someone who has sexual urges and feels sexual attraction towards other people. Some prefer it to the term allosexual as it doesn't originate from scientific terminology. It sounds less clinical and also implies a spectrum (from the 'a' of asexuality to the 'z' of zedsexual), which is more in line with progressive thinking on sexuality.

READING LIST

Ain't I a Woman
bell hooks

Bi: Notes for a Bisexual Revolution
Shiri Eisner

Britannia's Glory: History of Twentieth-century Lesbians
Emily Hamer

Coming Out
Jeffrey Weeks

Gay Life and Culture: A World History
Edited by Robert Aldrich

Good As You: From Prejudice to Pride – 30 Years of Gay Britain
Paul Flynn

How To Survive a Plague
David France

How to Understand Your Gender: A Practical Guide for Understanding Who You Are
Meg-John Barker, Alex Iantaffi

Purple Prose: Bisexuality in Britain
Kate Harrad

Queer: A Graphic History
Meg-John Barker
Illustrations Julia Scheele

The ABC's of LGBT+
Ashley Mardell

The History of Sexuality
Michel Foucault

The Invisible Orientation: An Introduction to Asexuality
Julia Sondra Decker

This Book is Gay
Juno Dawson

Transgender History
Susan Stryker

Trans Like Me
C N Lester

USEFUL LINKS

Adult LGBTQ+ Charities and Not-For-Profits
The charities included below are all national.
There may be some great charities that could
help you out in your local area.

FFLAG
www.fflag.org.uk

Galop
www.galop.org.uk

LGBT History Month
lgbthistorymonth.org.uk

MIND OUT
www.mindout.org.uk

Stonewall
www.stonewall.org.uk

The LGBT Foundation
http://lgbt.foundation

Youth LGBTQ+ Charities and Not-For-Profits
The charities included below are all national.
There may be some great charities that could
help you out in your local area.

Diversity Role Models
www.diversityrolemodels.org

Gendered Intelligence
http://genderedintelligence.co.uk

Imaan
https://imaanlondon.wordpress.com

LGBT Jigsaw
www.lgbtjigsaw.net

Mermaids
www.mermaidsuk.org.uk

NSPCC
www.nspcc.org.uk

Pink Therapy
www.pinktherapy.com

The Albert Kennedy Trust
www.akt.org.uk

The Happy Hippie Foundation
www.happyhippies.org

The Proud Trust
www.theproudtrust.org

Young Stonewall
www.youngstonewall.org.uk

NHS

Gender dysphoria
www.nhs.uk/conditions/gender-dysphoria

LGBT Health
www.nhs.uk/Livewell/LGBhealth/Pages/
Gayandlesbianhealth.aspx

Quick Guides

Spectrums:
https://en.wikipedia.org/wiki/Kinsey_scale
https://en.wikipedia.org/wiki/Klein_Sexual_
Orientation_Grid
https://en.wikipedia.org/wiki/Asexuality
http://gender.wikia.com/wiki/Gender_Wiki
http://sexuality.wikia.com/wiki/Sexuality_Wiki

If you're interested in finding out more about our books, find us on Facebook at **Summersdale Publishers** and follow us on Twitter at **@Summersdale.**

www.summersdale.com